Pembrokeshire Light

a collection of watercolours
by
Andrew Bailey

Published by Accent Press Ltd – 2006
ISBN 1905170327
Copyright © Andrew G Bailey 2006

The right of Andrew Bailey to be identified as the creator of this work has been asserted by him in accordance with the Copyright, Designs and Patents Act 1988. All rights reserved. No part of this book may be reproduced, stored in a retrieval system, or transmitted in any form or by any means, electronic, electrostatic, magnetic tape, mechanical, photocopying, recording or otherwise, without the written permission of the publishers: Accent Press Ltd, PO Box 50, Pembroke Dock, Pembrokeshire SA72 6WY.

Designed, printed and bound in the UK by Dimond Press, Well Hill, Pembroke, Pembrokeshire SA71 4DH Tel. 01646 682424.

I would like to thank my friends Martina and Gill and my son Rowan for their help and technical support during the time it took to pull this book together.

'View From Caerfai Bay, St Davids'   Map Ref. 1

There is a clear, pure quality to Pembrokeshire light. Artists have discussed and painted it for decades. Is it the clear air combined with large skies and low horizons, or the reflected light from the sea bounced high into the sky as the sun sets beyond it?

Two thirds of the Pembrokeshire coast faces west, an artist's dream as it produces a multitude of wonderful vistas just crying out to be painted: sunsets over the sea produce fantastic colours on the water and on wet sands. Low sun can cause glowing, back-lit waves the colour of barley sugar and silhouetted sea birds and islands. Gathering storms add their own colours and atmosphere and who can be unmoved by the hauntingly beautiful sight of sea mists rolling in off the Atlantic to muffle sounds and semi-obscure anchored boats.

The south of Pembrokeshire has equally breathtaking coastline features, such as Stack Rocks and Marloes Sands. The nearby Barafundle Bay was recently voted one of the top beaches in Britain.

The Coast

'Stackpole Mists'   Map Ref. 2

3

'Solva Harbour Mouth'

Map Ref. 3

To get this view walk over the left hand ridge or stay on the sand at low tide

'Tenby - Castle Beach'   Map Ref. 8

Above Left:
'Druidston Haven - The Afternoon Ride'

                                          Map Ref. 5

Left:
'Whitesands - Ramsey Sunset'

                                          Map Ref. 6

'Druidston Haven - Wet Sands'

Map Ref. 5

'Cast Upon the Sand'

Broad Haven

A popular stroll for locals and visitors alike is the walk on sand from Broad Haven to Little Haven at low tide. Broad Haven has the largest beach and village of the two and is recognisable by the Sphinx-like rock structure to the right, known as Lion Rock. It is a safe beach for children with plenty of rockpools to explore.

'What Is It? - Broad Haven'   Map Ref. 9

'After the Storm - Broad Haven'   Map Ref. 9

'Little Haven Point'

Map Ref. 10

'Little Haven - Spring Light'   Map Ref. 10   'Broad Haven - Lion Rock'   Map Ref. 9

8

'Rockpool Treasure'

Map Ref. 4

The fossil was found at Newgale and the treasure coin is wishful thinking!

Newgale

If you head north west from Haverfordwest to St Davids, your first sight of the sea will be at Newgale. A dramatic, wide strip of sand, three kilometres long at low tide. To the south are old coal seams, loved by fossil hunters, with huge cliffs that could have come out of a scene from "The Lost World". The sand finishes at Rickets Head and at this point it is possible to scramble up to the coastal path. To the north the beach continues past caves and tunnels to Peny Cwm. Driftwood and flotsam accumulates here and it is a rockpooler's dream. The view out to sea is equally dramatic with the whole sweep of St Brides Bay visible, the north and south terminating in the islands of Ramsey and Skomer.

'Newgale - Barley Sugar Waves'   Map Ref. 4   *'Newgale - Caught It!'*   Map Ref. 4

'Newgale - Evening Stroll'   Map Ref. 4

Left: 'Newgale - Look What I've Caught!'   Map Ref. 4

'Newgale - And the Sand Glowed!'   Map Ref. 4

Marloes Sands

Loved by geologists and artists alike, Marloes Sands is instantly recognisable by the jagged teeth of rock made up of diagonal bedding planes that intermittently jut up from the wide, sandy beach. To the right, Gateholm Island, still connected to the mainland at low tide, protrudes half a kilometre out to sea. Beyond is a glimpse of Skokholm Island, known by the Vikings as a land of ghosts because of the night time cries of Manx shearwaters. To the left is my personal favourite view of Marloes Sands. On a low tide it is possible to paint the dawn colours reflected on wet sands with the jagged teeth in silhouette.

'Marloes Sands - Storm Light'   Map Ref. 7

'Early Morning Walk - Marloes Sands'   Map Ref. 7

'Marloes Sands - Morning Light'

'Marloes Sands - Gateholm & Skokholm Islands'

'Stack Rocks - Storm Waves'

Map Ref. 11

Stack Rocks and the Green Bridge of Wales are both in an army firing range so check times for accessability.

'Barafundle Bay'　　　　Map Ref. 17

'Skokholm Island Bluebells'　　Map Ref. 13

'Ramsey Island Viewed From Whitesands'　　Map Ref. 14

'Skomer Gannets'　　Map Ref. 12

'Storm Ledge - Jack Sound - Opposite Skomer Island in the Deer Park'

Map Ref. 12

The Preseli Hills & Gwaun Valley

The land of stones, as I like to call it, the Preseli Hills to the north of Pembrokeshire, run east to west and are dotted with burial chambers and standing stones, the most famous of which is Pentre Ifan. The ridge path takes you past splintered, rocky outcrops such as Carn Menyn, the source of the bluestone used at Stonehenge. Often dark and brooding, the windswept hills must have been a special place for the ancient, celtic tribes of the area. In contrast, the Gwaun Valley, which runs along the feet of the Preselis is a sheltered, wooded place, gentle in nature with a beautiful river, the Afon Gwaun, that twists and turns its way through carpets of bluebells and ramsons in the spring. The steep-sided slopes of the valley are covered by ancient woodland and contain a series of hidden waterfalls, a lovely subject to paint, particularly with dappled light and sun rays through the leaves.

'Preseli Dawn'   Map Ref. 16

'Pool of Light - Gwaun Valley'

Map Ref. 15

This originally would have been covered by a mound of earth.

'Pentre Ifan - Preseli Hills'

'Trout Pool - Gwaun Valley'

Map Ref. 15

A tricky mad scramble over mossy boulders to find this spot.

'Preseli Hills - Spring Light'   Map Ref. 16

'The Rowan Pool'   Map Ref. 16

'Autumn Sun - The Gwaun Valley'   Map Ref. 15

'Sledging Day - Overlooking Rosebush Reservoir'   Map Ref. 16   *'Preseli Mists'*   Map Ref. 16

'Gwaun Valley Waterfall'   Map Ref. 15

Right: 'The Bluebell Path - Gwaun Valley'

Map Ref. 15

'The Stalwart Oak - Preseli Hills'   Map Ref. 16

22

Above: *'The Afon Gwaun - Gwaun Valley'*　　Map Ref. 15　　　　Below: *'Misty Oaks - Preseli Hills'*　　Map Ref. 16

'Bluebells'

'Snowdrops'

'Bramble Leaves'

Flora & Fauna

The unpolluted air, the coastal National Park and until recently, Pembrokeshire's remoteness has all helped to protect its flora and fauna.

The puffin is probably the most popular bird and it is possible to sit by their burrows, on the island of Skomer and have them walk right by you with a beakful of sand eels for their chicks. Dartford warblers are back in the county and choughs are now a common sight on the coastal path. Birdwatchers flock to the area alongside people who are whale and dolphin watching. The many boat trips around the islands give visitors the chance to see grey seals and harbour porpoises. On a fishing trip out to St Davids Head I was lucky enough to see an otter playing with a fish it had caught.

The high Pembrokeshire banks have an amazing variety of flora and fauna. The snowdrops in March run in a ribbon of white kilometre after kilometre in numbers I've not witnessed anywhere else. Rare orchids appear in Spring alongside primroses and cowslips which are then replaced by the taller wildflowers of the Summer, attracting many butterflies and providing shelter for lizards and slow worms.

'Bluebell Path'   Map Ref. 15

'Dryads Saddle'

'Primrose - Pembrokeshire Wildflowers'

25

26

'Fly Agaric'

'Choughs'

'Tawny Owl on Alder Stump'

'Gannets Find The Shoal - Ramsey Island'

Map Ref. 14

'Spring Fern and Marsh Marigold'

'Puffins - Skomer' Map Ref. 12

'Grey Seals - Ramsey Island'

Map Ref. 14

The best time to see seal pups is in September at Skomer, Ramsey Island or at The Dear Park, Martins Haven.

28

The St Davids Peninsula

The treacherous riptides of Ramsey Sound, numerous shipwrecks and stories of smuggling are all part of the character of the peninsula of St Davids. Add to this a beautiful cathedral, built in a hollow to prevent Viking raids, famous saints and stones, ancient burial chambers and hut circles and you have a place full of magic and mystery.

The two main beaches are Caerfai Bay and Whitesands. Caerfai is a more intimate place with striking red and blue coloured rocks that are quarried nearby for cathedral stone. Whitesands is a much wider beach with a stunning view across to Ramsey Island. The walk to St Davids Head passes ancient field systems, capped stones and a defensive wall called Warriors Dyke on the headland itself: a retreat for the Celtic tribe who once lived there.

'Caerfai Bay - Sparkling Water'   Map Ref. 1

'View From Carn Lliddi'   Map Ref. 6

'St Davids Head'

Map Ref. 6

A lovely walk from Whitesands Beach. Look out for hut circles in the last area of turf.

'St Davids Cathedral - Autumn Light!' Map Ref. 19

'Solva - Tranquil Waters' Map Ref. 3

'Whitesands Storm'

Map Ref. 6

'Whitesands Sunset'

Map Ref. 6

The view across to Ramsey Island from Whitesands Bay.

Mid County

'Over the Hedge - Blue Mists - Cardigan Road' Map Ref. 21

Right: 'Spring Mists - Cardigan Road, Haverfordwest' Map Ref. 21

Far Right: 'Cardigan Road Mists' Map Ref. 21

34

'Carew Castle'

Map Ref. 22

A dark stormy day until the sun, briefly broke through and produced this dramatic scene.

'Cleddau River'   Map Ref. 23

'Cleddau River - Rising Trout'   Map Ref. 24

'Cleddau Dawn - Treffgarne Gorge'   Map Ref. 24

This area can be found on the road from Haverfordwest to Fishguard

The Wildlife Garden

The garden is an important bolt hole for me. It helps recharge my batteries as I can only paint for two hours in one sitting and I then need a twenty minute break. Relaxing by the pond, watching the wildlife, keeps me going until the next field trip out to the woods or coast.

Starting with a waterlogged plot, due to compacted clay and very little top soil, I put in the most important features first: two ponds, native trees to break up the soil and nectar-rich plants to attract the insects. I have been inspired by it ever since.

'Crab Apple Blossom'

'Clematis'   *'Honeysuckle and Dog Rose'*   Snake's Head Fritillary